The Little Brown Dwarf That Could

Sherri Eisenhardt

BookLeaf Publishing

India | USA | UK

Presentation by *BookLeaf Publishing*

Web: www.bookleafpub.com

E-mail: info@bookleafpub.com

ISBN: 9789358310153

First edition 2023

DEDICATION

This book is for anyone that's ever felt like they aren't enough, too much, or both at the same time. Love bravely, loudly, and without apology. The world needs us as much as we need it.

This book is for little me, oh how I love her.

ACKNOWLEDGEMENT

My mom, as always, for being everything. Claude, for continuing to be my unpaid therapist. Em, for showing me it's ok to be selfish in the name of mental health. Judy, for sticking by me thru all of this. My dad, for sharing my accomplishments. It feels good to feel good.

PREFACE

This book is a collection of little things that have crossed my mind. They are a dissection of fleeting moments; good, bad, and indifferent. When I first started writing, I was afraid of people I know reading it because then they'd know how I feel. What a silly fear that is...

the fall

i am covered in
bruises.
i love them because
they are proof
of all the times i fell...
in love.

i am covered in
scars.
i love them because
they are proof
of all the times i thought i fell...
in love
but something else was there to catch me.

i have scraped knees
from being dragged
thru life by my heart
because it moves
quicker
than my feet.

here and gone

i want to be forgotten.
i want the last time
someone utters my name
to be on the first day
of spring.
i want the world to
get acquainted with
a life without my love
and then
i want it to cry
because
it really was
better with me in it.

self fulfilling martyr

because
that's what poets do;
they love
then
they lose

mobuis run away

the act of leaving
made me happy
but
when i got to where
i was going
i realized
i was just sad
in another place

light as a feather

in the real world
we have to escape our ribs
if we ever want
to survive being
in our heads.

in a better world
we have to escape
our heads if
we ever want
to survive
being in our ribs

war cry

i don't want to spend
the rest of my life
struggling to live it

what i've been up to

lately
i've been
minding my own business
and what i mean is
lately
i've been
laying in bed
writing books
bathing in nostalgia
for things
that haven't happened yet

cobwebs

if we wait for the right time
we may be waiting forever.
i may find myself
dusting cobwebs
from the corners
of the walls
that have heard
me say
i love you
thousands of times
as practice for
when the moment is right

i've never seen my mother
walk on water

i've never seen
my mother walk on water

but

i have seen her
wield love
like the last longsword in battle
and move mountains
with a flick
of her wrist

lighthouse vs lifeboat

i'm tired of loving
the void
for scraps of consciousness
but i love how
my light
reaches bravely
into the darkness

if the shoe fits

did it hurt?
when you searched
for yourself
in my pages
and
saw no evidence
of your existence?

untitled #2

picking up
my teeth is
acknowledging
how many times
the truth has
fallen out
of my mouth
in front of you.
and now it's
the only motivation
i have to
keep my mouth
closed

just in time for mason jar memories

are his hand a little worn?
do they fold perfectly into mine?
and when he leans in
to kiss me...

do i pretend
that he looks at my photos
and wonders how ever
went so long without me?
does his messy brown hair
and sleepy eyes
wearing a side smile
scream
"this means a lot to me?"

will he laugh
at all the empty coffee cups
strategically placed
around my bedroom?
will he hate how
certain books
collect dust?
not because i don't clean them
but because i don't pick them up enough

what i mean when i say bare bones

love is
showing you
my skeleton
after i've
washed off
all the glitter

depressed vs deep rest

my bed wins more times
than i care to admit

and on those days
when the truth
is stuck in my throat
and i'm reduced to
a sad, hollow skin

i sleep
and sleep
and sleep
and sleep

free will

fate is
overrated.
love me
on purpose.

my severance package is melancholy

the overwhelming pain
that comes from releasing your old self
and realizing it's the hardest bond to break,
the most painful experience because
she is who got you here.
the survival mode
the primal instinct
the fight
the pick me back up
the dust me off
the keeps-coming-back-for-more
with
the wild in her eyes
and scars on her face

she is the warrior
the strength
the beat in my chest
the battle cry
and distant war drum

but
she does not know how to
be gentle

be kind
be soft

and in a world that is
woefully lacking in safe places
i needed to become one

not a home for broken hearts
just a lighthouse in a storm
holding the mirror up
when the world tries
to wash you away

and knowing i will never be a home

hurts.

i foster the lost
i love outcasts
i harness the wild in the palms of my hand
until they realize
they've always been able to fly

oh, to be love
and never know its face

if i died right now

realizing i have only
30 or 40 summers left
makes it sound like
life is too short
and i want it to
be...
longer.

thinking about
all of the moments
i will miss,
all of the candles
i won't get to blow out,
all the
scrapes
and cuts
and bruises
i won't get to kiss,
all of the
books i won't read
art i won't make
music i wont hear
food i wont't eat
the laughs i'll miss
and times i'm needed but can't help.

all the love i have
is what i want to leave.

it makes me wonder
if i'm powerful enough
to push thru the
folds of time
to be there when
they reach for me

christmas list

one day i want to say
i'm doing okay
and really mean it.
i want to say their names
with the same glow
i had before.
i want to wake up
in warmth.
i want to know that
not every day
is a funeral.
when we say
rest in peace,
i want to really feel it.
i want to shake off
the fear
of last breaths
and find comfort
in my own mortality.
i want to know that
this hurt isn't forever.

long nights

i don't know how
to only scratch the surface.
i am unsatisfied
with topical pleasantry exchanges.
a lack of depth is
suggestive to many things.

i want to see more
than this scope of light.
i want to witness
the tendrils that connect us.
i want to lose sight
of the space between.

i want the things
said to the air around me
to snag on clothes and
pull us back to now.
i want thoughts
to hang crooked like neglected frames,
as if to scream in desperation,
the need to be noticed.
i want to lose self control
because it's
the only thing
holding me back.

run, leap, fall, repeat

"you will be forgotten
at an astonishing pace"
use this information wisely.
and selfishly.
and bravely.
if it doesn't
make you feel the pounding in your chest,
find things that will.
and chase them
as if your life depends on it.

* 9 7 8 9 3 5 8 3 1 0 1 5 3 *